T0040484

Herod's Dispensations

HEROD'S DISPENSATIONS

Harry Clifton

WAKE
FOREST
UNIVERSITY
PRESS

First North American edition

© Harry Clifton, 2019

For permission, write to

Wake Forest University Press

Post Office Box 7333

Winston-Salem, NC 27109

WFUPRESS.WFU.EDU

WFUPRESS@WFU.EDU

ISBN 978-1-930630-87-1 (*paperback*)

Library of Congress Control Number 2018953252

Designed and typeset in Dante

by Nathan Moehlmann,

Goosepen Studio & Press

Publication of this book was generously supported

by the Boyle Family Fund

CONTENTS

ACKNOWLEDGMENTS

Acknowledgments are due to *The Stinging Fly, Poetry East, The Irish Times, The Stony Thursday Book, The Poetry Review, The Manhattan Review, The Times Literary Supplement, Temenos, Poetry Ireland Review, Poetry Salzburg Review, Icarus, The High Window, Reading the Future* (Arlen House), *The Dublin Review of Books,* Qualm website, and Stoney Road Editions where some of these poems first appeared.

Herod's Dispensations

TO THE NEXT GENERATION

These days, like the leech-gatherer
In Wordsworth, I keep the wolf from the door
Of indigence, and take the weather
On the lonely moor.

The gibbet creaks in the wind. The body is gone.
Here comes a soldier, home from the war.
Napoleon, he tells me, is no more,
The work of healing is done

And the million sutures closed, below on the plain
Where the bloods are drawn.
I ask myself private questions now, in the dawn,

About women and poems, the impossibilities
Of old age, dipping for pondlife in the rain
As a child looks up to me.

REDESDALE ESTATE, 1956

for Catriona Crowe

First, this old clock. As I dismantle it,
A child of indeterminate age
On the garage floor, the cogs and flywheels
Buzz, the hour-hands race and stop,
Go back on themselves,
And I peer, like a little god,
In the workings of time. Steady,
The ticking starts, suburban days
Falling into place
Like memory. Glass front doors
And front room windows
Are black depths, to be looked into
Afterwards, when the time is right.
But for now, each pebbledashed house
Is a Freudian box of tricks,
Pre-conscious, locked in itself,
Respectable, safe, like Nineteen Fifty Six.

Pounds and ounces, pennyweights and grams —
A grocer's measuring instruments
Sift reality, slicing ham
And butter, trowelling sugar in brown paper bags
For all of us blow-ins, on whom the hag
Has roosted, the hag of Ireland,
Stateless... Lord Redesdale,
Whoever you were, you gave us the myth of a State,

You left us your name
To conjure with, on your sold estate,
And fled to England, clutching the deeds.
De Valera set us down here, and bade us breed.

A new generation. A clean slate
For history to write on. Non-attachment
Our middle name. Sleepless, we hear
The cattle-drive, to the milking-sheds
Of Stillorgin, in the early hours,
Like the lost morning of a mythic race
Our fathers snore through. De Valera,
Give us our pasteurized milk, and cleanse our blood
Of impurities. Banish the gypsy horses,
Their mounds of fertile dung,
From our gardens. Tinsmiths' fires
Will burn themselves out, the caravan train move on —
Give us leave to live here...
                    O the pain
That first winter of consciousness —
Snowballs, tainted with copper sulphate,
Crash against my ears. The Zen command
To awaken! Child, it is too late
To run in tears to Mother.
She points to the orphans, filing through the estate
From nowhere to nowhere, shadowed by Sisters
Terrible in their winged headgear
Out through the age of innocence, into the years
Undreamt by De Valera, Connolly, Pearse.

ENDGAME

The old fog calls
        — Samuel Beckett

I never belonged in my father's house—
His unread Bible on the shelf
My silent coming of age.
In the kitchen, pregnant pauses,
Whispering. Behind pages
Of the *Irish Times*, the man himself

Hiding from Ireland in Ireland.
People used to call,
I remember, in the old days—
Musical instruments, coats in the hall,
Sectarian difference, shouting. Trays
Of edibles, hand to hand,

As once in Joyce's *Dubliners*.
I ask myself now, would I want it all back.
Anything but, in the name of Krapp.
A hundred houses, back to back
Against nothingness. Foghorn-blur
In Dublin Bay, as a ship

From Liverpool or Holyhead
Reversed through time into history.
The shouting has stopped, the whispering
In the kitchen has died away.
I lift to my eye instead
The spyglass in the Beckett play

And see, through the matte grey
Of a Sunday afternoon
Without God, Dun Laoghaire
In focus, millions on a pier—
Those who can never do themselves in,
Those who can never pray.

THE ACCURSED QUESTIONS

1

The girl behind the bar is in love with you, do you know that?
Look at what happened to Kierkegaard, Dostoyevsky —
Sad lives, early deaths, the world no better a place.

It is cold in the kitchen, but you feel nothing,
Reading… The Russians, too, never felt their own weather
In all those fictions. It came from inside them.

People out walking, on the East Pier,
Swarm in their thousands, ghosts of the Nevsky Prospekt.
Where do they come from? Where on earth do they vanish to?

2

Grey-haired now, the girl behind the bar
Has given up on children… And for forty years
No one has disturbed it, the white cold silence of the kitchen.

The bollards are still grass-grown, on that other pier
Across the water, where time stops
And a decommissioned lightship rusts at anchor.

Half the world has gone to its death. But you,
You are still eighteen, the ice on the Neva
Still unbroken, life unreal outside the hermitage wall.

AFTER MAO

Her beauty was cold to the touch
Like marble. She was not there
In flesh or spirit. Two or three words
In a foreign tongue, and the rest
Silence. On she worked,
Ignoring her own nakedness,
Her slavery skin-deep and her dream
Off limits. And the streets
Outside, the city cold around her,
Night growing out of nowhere.

Money and strange hours, a room.
There was a train once, through China—
Father to Mother, out of which grew
Like a taproot, singlemindedness,
Detachment, lights in passing,
Distances…
                    That country
Is everywhere, its separations
Early, its children turned to stone.

ACROSS THE RIVER

I crossed them again, the Liffey
And the Lethe, and there it all was,
The seventies, north of the river,
Nothing changed. The smells of food,
The same lit pubs, with a failed generation
Drinking inside them, in a blue fug
Clinging to the loose-stitch and the breast-swell
Of a girl's pullover, who would go on
To age, make children,
Break with the crises, the excitements
Of Saturday night, for the grey of Sunday afternoon.

There were no more Sundays now
But I smelt the docks, on the farther side of Lethe,
The ghosts of the transit sheds
For cattle and emigrants, shipped to Liverpool—
Abbatoir of souls…

Local color, raised to the power of infinity
Once, long ago. Back then,
Staring much, I saw too little.
Now, a gull might cut right through me
For all I knew, and everything be remembered
Out of nowhere, the city reassemble itself
From the ruins of the seventies,
I its soul-survivor,

And the bad poetry, the only real poetry,
Still being sold, from an upstairs loft
On Middle Abbey street, by a dropout
From the future, loose-stitched, heavy-breasted,
Careless of second comers. Mnemosyne,
Daughter of memory.

RUINS

A thought of that late death
Took all my heart for speech

— W. B. Yeats

My generation, dropping like flies —
At least in Stalingrad
There were ruins, a battleground.
Here, the buildings rise,
The minds collapse. As John of God
Slides by, a halfway house

For the saint, the suicide
And the family sacrifice,
I stay in lane, in the living tide
Of windscreens and car-bonnets,
Deaf to the silent cries,
The incoming round with my name on it.

The offensive has begun.
A woman walked into the sea
Just yesterday. A man was hung,
Self-hung, from the hook of desertion
There behind suburban curtains,
Disbelieving in victory.

Anne and David, Geraldine —
Enough that I drive by
Once in a while, at the violet hour
Of medication, Gethsemane hour
For the hero, the heroine.
Let me leave you where you lie

Undecorated, even by God,
The children of a neutral state
Who went down fighting, hand to hand,
With your own shadows, self-destroyed,
Caught in the suction of the void
That let the city stand.

DAYTIME SLEEPER

A Shanghai night-poet
Keeping Chinese hours
Looks across the lights of Dublin
At the sleeping powers

On western time. A little wine
But mostly tea, exfoliating
Leaf by strange green leaf
In earth-dark, where the soul alone

Drinks to itself in the windowpane.
After Mao, the masses, slaughter,
Brotherless, the lonely daughter
Of the Policy of One

Is staring out, through bloodshot eyes,
At emptiness a Trappist monk
Might waken to, and never blink
In time or history. O for advice

From that strange soul-sister
Out of Asia, someone new,
A veteran of Anabasis,
A follower of Chuang Zhu,

A Gnostic at the hour of sex
Who sees through all the books…
She must be sleeping by now,
Her hair cut straight across her brow,

Her dregs brewed out, her left brain's
Dreaming mind a hemisphere
Ahead of me, already night
In Shanghai as I write.

THE EGG-WIFE

Mainly remembered for the wind that blew
Beneath her door, as the negotiations,
Not difficult, continued... Sheepdogs too,
Barking, whimpering for admission

From the big cold, the distances outside,
The hinterlands. How it would be in winter
We could imagine — Aga stove at center,
Two small children taken in her stride...

Egg-whites, spreading evenly on a pan,
Their yolks unbroken (ours the brokenness).
Telegraph poles, an infinite succession

Over the skyline. Somewhere about, her man,
And flesh as grass in the wind, that summer day —
Hardly selling, giving her eggs away.

THERESE AND THE JUG

Marriage is the monastery of our time

— Leonard Cohen

She liked the jug, because it was cracked.
If it had a flaw
It was perfect. Under God's law
It was made whole by what it lacked—

Or so you tell me, matter of fact,
As you water a whisky
Last thing at night, or sweeten Darjeeling tea
With the milk and honey of tact.

How many decades now
Since we entered the enclosed order
Of ourselves, to raid and replenish the larder
Of imperishables? The marriage vow

Grown ordinary, seems to keep house
And break bread with us, through and through,
At communal vespers for two
Like a hidden spirit. Patient Therese,

Our patron saint of the infinitely small,
Examines the wedding plunder, stainless steel,
Anything bedsheets might reveal
The morning after... Total recall,

If it ever came, would be shattering as a mirror
We stand before daily,
Man and wife, success and failure —
Childless love, imperfect as a marriage

Or that fissured jug, its flaw that integrates
A world around it, so you say,
A world left behind, for the Little Way
Of ovulins and fetherlites.

BEFORE CHRIST

She left me a tax letter, on the table.
Deal with that, she said. Unopened,
Unread, it lay there, hours on end.

Something Roman, I said to myself,
Sent from another realm, to bleed us dry,
The people of the spirit, her and I.

A name, a telephone number. Yellow paper,
Dry, official. I would never get through
To anyone real, with my unresolved question.

Nor would it go away. Like Caesar
Or the State, a moving shadow
As the pen moves, the shadow of a hand,

A man and his shadow, co-writing,
Simultaneous, in invisible ink,
Two histories, of Israel and of Rome.

How many massacres, I wondered,
Deserts and messiahs, Herods, Pilates,
Tax collectors with inviolate souls

Had it taken, for this privileged trance
I lay back into, abdicating everything,
To exist? *No answer necessary*

I might have told her, at eleven,
As she left, through the extra-temporal door.
Now, as I finish this, it is almost four.

A FLIGHT INTO EGYPT

Sixteen years we lived among alien people,
Cities without bridges to be burned,
Uncertain roofs—protecting ourselves, a couple
Gone into hiding, who would one day return
When the balance of power changed, and the attitudes.
Meanwhile, strangers were kind. The terrible places,
Unexpectedly, were generous with food,
Indifferent for the most part, sometimes even gracious.
And to this day, our books on the shelf,
Our suitcases unpacked, I ask myself
If ever it might happen again—
Protection of innocence, Herod's dispensations,
Transit lounges, midnight railway stations—
No, not even whether, only when.

PITY AND TERROR

Whoever they are, they hate it. They're afraid—
   The man of foreign extraction
In the second row, and the woman beside him
Out of Ardmore studio, following the action,
Clutching his elbow. "…Die, you shagging bitch,
Or take off back to Crewe across the water—
Do you hear me?" Listening, the daughter
Backs towards the audience, stopping barely an inch

Beyond the double glaze of pity and terror,
   The pair of them.
Again the voice of a mother, through the terrible mirror
Held to the nation. "What did you ever care
For Irish freedom?… Your father, the I.R.A.…."
A trembling hand pours tea, from a real pot,
In mythic space. A distant radio plays.
They're dreaming of the interval, like as not,

That mystery couple… Sure enough, it arrives,
   The space of enlightenment
Everyone here has swung for, in a previous life—
The liberal buzz and murmur, Synge's rioters
Gone quiet for an age, between the acts,
In changing motley, waiting. Her and him
The interval bell as certainly drags back
To earlier darkness, as the lights again grow dim

On old age propped on pillows, tea turned gin,
  A table set for one.
Will anything change? Will anyone burst in
From a better world "Oh Christ, I thought you were gone…"
To work white magic? Lonely on a wall
The lights of a passing car. And time crawls,
The daughter listens again. "That radio,
Turn it off… It was all such a long, long time ago…"

And no, they do not like it. They're afraid,
  Wishing themselves in bed,
Far into each other, a million miles away
On the other side of Abbey Street, Burgh Quay,
Bursting through traffic and rainfall,
Grimed cafes and savage pubs, and the laws
Of iron necessity, to a curtain-call
Beyond Ireland, a freedom without applause.

ART, CHILDREN AND DEATH

I love only art, children and death

— Alexander Blok

A literary man blows in from Cork
On literary business. Glad of a chat
In the lonely hour between the end of work
And the railway station. This and that—
Divorces, second families, his book
And the pasting it took in last week's *Irish Times,*
And still, one goes on writing... Coffee, talk,
The long perspective. Some day, when it comes,
There will be no one, in the latening roar
Of an age that passes. Only Heuston Station—
Transients, plastic tables, paper plates,
The crumbs of controversy, reputation—
Only the provinces, out past Inchicore,
The children's children, and the train that waits.

DISFAVOR

I, Heinrich Heine,
No longer or not yet
In favor, decline
In this lazaret

Of Paris, attended
By a peasant childwife,
Her infantile mind
Still believing in love.

Outside, no greenery,
Only a street.
Serves you right,
The Volk would say,

For heaping ironies
On our Black Forest trails,
Our darkness, in *Harzreise,*
Germany: A Winter's Tale.

Alone among German poets,
The critics harangue
Me, you never wrote
A decent drinking-song.

And those I defamed
Disown me, withhold
My inheritance.
Changing my name

From Harry to Heinrich,
I try assimilation.
No good, in the current mood—
Cosmopolitan! Stinkjude!

Disintegration
Of the lower spine—
Six mattresses
Support you, Heine,

More than the rise of nations.
You were never one of us,
They tell me. Your country
For you, is syphilis,

The tertiary stage.
Deaf to the call
Of a new, heroic age,
I turn my face to the wall,

Prefer disease
And living women
To the kiss of death,
The anthologies.

London, 1992

THE STAGE-DOOR

Neary's, Chatham Street

They slipped out the back, through the stage-door,
Cut in here. Old bottles, lining the shelves,
Tobacco-smoke, the noise... For half an hour
They could be their real selves

As I remember them, with the greasepaint off.
Always the actor must fail
In the last performance, coat-trailing,
Legless, having his cough

Loosened, his pockets shaken down...
I watched, invisible for years
Up here in the gods, as the laughter-drowned,
The tragic, the cast in order of appearance

Burnt themselves out, like the legendary gas lamps
Along the counter—growing into my role
Of opera phantom, prompter through a hole
At Method, Stanislavsky or High Camp,

Only needing words and whisky-breath,
An art-girl or a leap of faith,
An interval, a space between the acts
To contemplate the truth, if not the facts.

THE ACHILL YEARS

If the Greeks experienced despair, it was always
through beauty and its oppressive quality

— *Albert Camus*

1

Graham, Paul and Robert, lost at sea
Between dreams of art and a weekly farmer's market,
Pedaling into the wind for all these years,
And Louis too, and Mannie, warped like trees
Outside each others' windows, in the mind-darkening
Onset of Atlantic drizzle, pocking the Ice Age lakes—
You're only the latest... Take yourselves to bed
Or leave forever. Either way, bring food
For an island interlude, where the spirit breaks
Like whisky on the rocks, in the Hotel Amethyst,
Waiting for clearance, and the high blue days
Of space into vertigo, vertigo into space—
Everyone else half-drunk on Irish mist,
Stumbling home, through a world of appearances.

2

The disconnect with the landscape,
The vacuum, you would say,
From man to nature, far Dooega
Through to Dookinella,
Brings out the drinker in each of you.

You are sucked out, like an egg,
Through your own eyes
Into azures, greys,
Which, if you understood them
Properly, would be horrors of a kind.

And yet, you stay on the island,
Painting. Years pass
Unchanging, the mountains in the distance,
The sea at hand, the canvases
Accumulating,

Priceless, worthless.
Others, trying too hard to see,
Get drunk on air, and shoot themselves
From loneliness, despair —
The huge inscrutability,

The island, with its question.
Words are too social,
Too intimate. All eye, no mind,
Where the anti-poet thrives,
Is what survives.

HORACE

That most vulgar of crowds the literary

—*John Keats*

Sick of that bloody poet, everywhere
Smart casual, urbane and circumspect,
Choosing his words with a little too much care
To be real anymore, command respect
Or say a single thing worth listening to,
It came to me the only road to go
(Not martyrdom) was sheer, deliberate death
Made to seem like accident—too slow
To be suicide, too chaotic for myth
To be shaped of it afterwards. Satires? Odes?
No, silence. And the Roman gods
Discredited, through whose eyes,
At too many wine receptions, weighing the odds,
I watched the art of perfect compromise.

THE BIBLE AS LITERATURE

In a locked, upper room,
For the authorities were about,
The disciples waited. And Christ came —
On his hands, his feet,

The stigmata. Transpierced
His side, where blood and water,
(Suffering innocence)
Issued, just for the record.

On the agenda, one item —
The impossible. Was it the wall
He had come through, or the window,
Breathing, passing along

The knowledge beyond death,
The leap of faith
Involved, from here on out,
In getting up in the morning,

Going about the business of the world?
There were stones to be etched,
New lectors to amaze. A day
Might supervene, or ageless centuries,

Before He, who had floated out
The window, floated back in again
With the ending to the Book.
Meanwhile, *vox populi*

And the literary games—
False messiahs, brought in chains
From Antioch all the way to Rome,
Dying to make their names.

AT RACQUETS

Let's play hardball. Hamlet and Horatio
Back from Wittenberg, Laertes in from Paris —

Fencing, sex, and fallings-out at tennis,
At the sagging net of an outer court,

The heart of a long-lost summer... Politics,
Power, return us to Denmark. Watch us leap and smash

In chalk-marked space, a court within a court,
A play within a play, as fathers, mothers,

Drift onstage, for the fifth act
And the pile of corpses — venoming foils

For the sons already wounded, too far gone
For school debate, who dropped out

Long ago, with points to score
In love and war, on either side of the question.

THE PIT

One by one, you are led to the pit
And in you stare, at all those gone before you,
Naked, splayed on top of each other,
Caught in their last wild grimace. Who would spare you?
No one, nothing. Somewhere Holy Writ,
This day, in Heaven, thou shalt see thy Father—
Doubled up, they laugh at your distress,
The executioners… Knowledge without bitterness,

Is that what you were promised? Piles of clothes,
Belongings. Loved remembered images,
Still or moving. Time accelerated,
Hair gone grey. To remember, to suppose,
Irrelevant now. Your cities still undamaged,
Streets of a different epoch. Loved and hated
Men and women, scorch-marks on a wall,
Shadows, from an age before the Fall.

Millions of flies have settled everywhere
Once, long ago. Our urns, our ashes, laughable
To you now, and our neighborhoods
Deathless. You would say how lucky we are,
Unimaginable, in our future, beyond the rubble
Of cities, the battles of bad and good,
The categories—our mortgage on existence
Year by year, our time without history,

Everything rebuilt, a simulacrum
Of the real, a street of haunted people
Drawn together by intangible fear,
Meeting like lovers, under the steeples
Of a deconsecrated church — our Kingdom Come
Each other, our heavens blue and clear,
Our past eradicated, in the pit,
Our deaths that never come, our ruins lit.

WRECKFISH

As a wreckfish cruised
I imagined it, fathoms underwater,
At large in the real blue

Of the human catastrophe,
Not this tanked aquarium light,
These people, oxygenated.

Bones of armadas
White as a ribcage
Glided through, and picked-off insights

Tiny as snails… A go-between
In half-lit worlds, insurance,
Undertaking. A loner

Among shoals, in the clockwork surf
Exploding on fake reefs,
With nowhere to dive to,

Nothing to resurrect —
A twenty-pounder
Among minnows, circling blindly

In its mirled dimension,
Bubble-hiss, too long in the tooth
For our million years,

Our trivia. Hull-haunter,
Soul-monger, slowing me down
To the sluggish beat

Of its cold-blooded heart,
Inhabiting me, as I moved between
Disaster, salvage, art.

THE DRY-SOULED MAN

Yvor Winters, 1900–1968

1

Where you end up, in the boiler basement room
Of Stanford faculty, Professor X
Who never lived, who thinks he knows Crane's poems,
Can't get to you. The staff of '66

Are shacking up with students, getting stoned
In hope of tenure. Listen, planes up there —
American self-belief, and its counter-tone,
Soul music. California grows long hair,

Undresses, wanders nude in its own parks
Through jasmine weather, Emersonian highs,
Haight Ashbury, Berkeley… far overhead, the B-52s
For Vietnam. "I'm sorry Winters, your work

Is a disgrace to this department…" Kennedy said
In that chairman's office, long ago.
Kennedy, and how many millions, are dead.
Droning in close formation, even now

His demons thrive, in the moist-damp atmospheres
Of south-east Asia, the "blood-smell of prey"
As Saint Augustine says. The demons of emotion —
Waves of amplified sound, Pacific oceans…

2

Now, so near retirement, past all that,
A desert lies behind you. Santa Fe—
Your sick young self, in quarantine on the plateau
Of New Mexico, under a rainless sky,

All day long to write and drink, in shacks
Of blue adobe, towns without streetcar lines,
Sleep with dark *mestizas*, the daughters of copper mines,
Recover your rhythm, get your breathing back.

Someone or something is there, outside the door.
Is it Professor X? Or is it Crane
Back from the underworld, like Orpheus?
"Winters, for all your talk of the dry-souled man

You need a drubbing..." Silence, it's too late
To change conviction now. Pacific mist
From Pasadena to the Golden Gate
Rolls in like tear gas, and the campuses are lost

To the long-hair ideologues. Remote, archaic,
The dangerous years of poetry, bad sex
And playing with fire. Today, the pride of the stoic
In his own endurance—secular crux,

Dry measure, as the bombers drone overhead
And the beat goes on. Outside that basement room—
Your *Forms of Discovery* stacked on shelves, unread—
The unmistakable sweep of an iron broom.

TRANCE

1

Somebody said "There's a job going
In Africa..." And the next thing

I was on that plane. Which year?
I don't remember. *You are here*

Said the map, and that was enough.
I taught some classes, fell in love

And watched a government collapse.
Savannahs, storms, cross-country trips,

Alone not lonely in a Volks,
Through a wilderness of withering stalks...

The wide blue sky, the laterite belt—
Everything seen and nothing felt.

2

Somebody said "There are children dying
In Asia..." And the next thing

I was on that plane. Don Muang—
Americanized. Simon and Garfunkel sang

Through tannoy, at the shakedown points.
The camps, the women rolling joints

Are all I remember. Blazing food
For jaded palates. And the giving of blood

Up-country, in a lying-down faint,
And coming-to, a secular saint

With lives in my hands, long working hours
And a dreamy feeling of power.

3

Everything heatstruck, in a trance —
Adrenaline, auto-immune defense,

Fantastic overcompensation
Roaming the earth, and saving nations,

Touching down in my own backyard
With a jolt and a mocking word,

A blow from a Zen instructor's wand,
And slowly, slowly coming round

Through days and years, in patient rooms,
To the self as home from home,

To nearness, touch, the strength to feel,
To the limited, to the real.

AUDEN IN SHANGHAI

Okay, you wrote one sonnet. In between,
Poetry in abeyance. Afternoon flings
In the bath-house — Chiang, the local scene.
For who would want to read about such things

In Nineteen Thirty Eight, with the opium wars
Turned ideological, and the Japanese
Hovering? Off to the Front then, in closed cars,
Where no one sees, through the smoke of generalities,

Your one dead Chinese soldier... Decades on,
The ghost of Chiang, with therapeutic oil,
A person not a category, someone real

With a home to go to, and real needs,
Massages you. Don't ask him what he reads
If he ever did, or which side ever won.

ANABASIS

Saint-John Perse, Peking 1917

Forbidden to the city, looking out
Beyond Mongolia, lies the hinterland
Of imagination. Watchtower and redoubt,
The lost Qing dynasties, are grass in the wind.
Gone the binary world of time and place,
The Occident, the Orient, interchangeable —
Pieces in a chessgame... On he plays
With Liang Kichao, with Liu. Already the Stranger

Forms inside him, like a pure idea —
He who writes the book of yellow dust,
Who contemplates the ends of civilizations,
The beginnings... Of all hours, these the happiest
While the stable-boy from the Legation
Grooms his desert stallion, tamed before the Fall,
And tree frogs, a mosquito off the wall
Perch at his plate, a woman pours green tea

And the epic goes on forming. *Anabase —*
The movement of peoples, after Xenophon,
To and from the ocean...
                              Here inland
The northwest wind. She lights the Russian stove
In the winter garden, where a lizard plays
At killing insects, and the War goes on.
Liang Kichao has moved. A counter-move
From Liu Tsiang-tsen. Outside, blown sands

Of plague, oblivion, warlords at the gate.
Tomorrow to set up a quarantine.
Tomorrow Li and his hundred concubines
To be sheltered here, in this state within a state,
The diplomatic zone… Minutiae,
Duties. Let the real thing grow
Inside, where no man sees it. Lei Hi-Gnai
His chessmates call him. Thunder beneath the Snow.

And some day, come the summer, he will go
Behind the veil of time and history
Where the gods lie around, in smashed theogonies
Of stone, to sleep in the ruins of Tao-Yu
And wake to the human caravan setting out
All over again, forever going west —
The wild geese flying, absence of whereabouts,
Mountain cold, an epic space as vast

As Inner Mongolia, setting itself free.
By the roads of all the earth, the Stranger to his ways…
The child of an island race, in the Gulf Stream,
Who sees it all already in a dream
(Gone the binary world of time and place).
The horse on the desert route, who scents the sea
And dies inland. The son without a mother
Grown into a man eternally other

Sleeping under the stars, in high Xinchan
Tonight, Beijing in the distance, incoming flights,
Thalassal surge of traffic, avenues of lights…
Here comes the boy, from the other side of time,
With eggs, a pullet, legends of Verdun,
The boy from the stables, beating a little stone drum
Below by the river, for the ferry across
From Tiananmen Square to Xenophon's wilderness.

from RED EARTH SEQUENCE

1. The Mouth of the Yangtze

All that flying time at body heat —
And now at last descent... The spirit-worlds
Of Sichuan, Tibet, have drained away
To shipping lanes and Japanese defeat,
Drowned Studebakers, yesterday's bar-girls,
Gold teeth gone, who walked the Shanghai streets
In Nineteen Forty Five and saw the flash
Five hundred miles away — Hiroshima
Or the end of the world... If time, eternity
Ever meet, tomorrow or today,
My criminal essence and my need to pray
Will break apart on impact, in the South China Sea,
Or make it through, on a wing and a prayer
To a deathless landing. No one will meet me there.

2. The Life on Zentong Street (for Huiyi Bao)

Smell it, the osmanthus. Heavy, sweet,
The essence of China, as the poet once said.
For days I hang out here, on Zhentong Street,
Making a world, recovering, lightheaded

After time zones. Children, break my heart
For childlessness. Street-women, sprawl at ease
On your public sofa. Life has beaten art,
The innocence and the sleaze.

The vulcanizer's spark, the cobbler's awl
Monopolize the empire, great in small.
Laughter claps a hand to its own mouth

In pure embarrassment at the power of mood.
Past the point of beauty, short of death,
Never does plain water taste so good.

3. Autumn in Chengdu

At the slightest rain, a flowering of umbrellas
Fourteen stories down. The human sea,
The "ocean of suffering," or so they tell me—
Deaths, rebirths... How many days now, all alone
At the heart of reality, in the white noise
Of a jammed radio, the fuzz on the internet,
Do I cut myself off, the better to atone
For ever living? It is not time yet
For the leaves that never fall, on the trees of Chengdu—
But the cripples and the hydrocephalic boys
At the Buddhist gates, the lama's cry
On the loudspeaker, powerfully coming through
The smog of appetite, are reaching me
Even now, and teaching me to die.

4. At the White Night Café

A poet of the Meo tribe, smoking weed,
Ignores me, ostentatiously. Ms. Zhai
With a hand-held camera, looks herself in the eye.
"It is time, now, for our honored guest to read."

Professor Chan sits down. I see John Wong
Stealing, surreptitiously, anything he is able,
From the uncleared plates on the revolving table.
Xu translates. A travesty, all wrong—

But who will care? The smoke and mirrors, drinks,
The zither-pluckings ancient as Du Fu,
The spot-lit stage, projectionist on cue,

Inspired misunderstandings, age to age,
Are crowding in on me, as the stone page
Turns, I clear my throat, and darkness blinks.

5. Red Earth

Huge as China, tiny as a door
To a higher incarnation... No one there
To meet me, no one to say goodbye.
Such is the infinite courteousness, I could die
On the wrong side of language. Where I go
There is only silence. Everywhere, crowded floors
Of airports, Himalayan air
In the distance, or the nearness of gingko trees —
Mongolian space, the nomad's empty stare
In total externality. Two currencies,
Origin, destination, burn a hole
In my pocket, whatever each is worth.
Meanwhile, the body in transit. And the soul
Eternally foreign, vaster than red earth.

ZHOUKOUDIAN

Praise to you harsh matter, which one day will be dissolved
with us and carry us into the heart of Reality

— Teilhard de Chardin

1929

We were digging deep in time, towards nightfall,
A light snow falling, and the journey back
To Peking ahead of us, when the spade struck
Something in the matrix. "Davidson Black,"
Said Pei, "will want to see it all..."
So we axle-cranked that travertine of rock

By rail-line forty long kilometers
To the Cenozoic Lab. Where Black, that night,
Would cancel his engagements, I remember —
All that klieg-lit world of socialites,
Fowl and oyster feastings through December,
Winter palaces and glib ice-skaters —

Chipping away, with dental instruments,
At the myth of creation, the dogma of the Pope,
While Teilhard, who would hang by his own rope
Of Catholic heresy, watched the protuberant
Forebrain coming clear, as the human ape
Of Zhoukoudian, the one in a billion chance,

The stealer of fire, the ghost in the machine,
Sinanthropus, or Peking Man,

The heresy for which nothing can atone
But death of temple, church, the image of Christ
In smithereens, the bible turned to dust —
Unearthed itself in each of us alone.

2016

Was I there? Am I here tonight,
A soul-abandoned body hearkening back
From Dongshimen district, to the ghost of Black,
The old hostesses? Pei the Japanese shot,
And Teilhard died, a pastor without flock
In a New York room — anathema, frozen out,

The founder, so they say, of his own religion,
Gnosis… In the zone of institutes,
Embassies, and the flags of nation-states,
The massage-parlors glow, and the winter kitchens
Billow cooking-smoke from the street below.
The skull unsocketed, that never nictates,

Sees everything, at all hours. Through the wall
A woman wild as wind off Asian steppes
Empties her bladder in the toilet-bowl
Of the unholy. No Creation, no Fall —
A man in the background swearing, a question of tips.
I stand on the bathroom scales and weigh my soul

By its only law—true matter. Co-religionist,
Gnostic, heretic, Teilhard, I,
As the spirit in my shot-glass drinks itself dry
In dehydration, drink to his lonely ghost
Out there in the Beijing night—and the rise of Man,
The death of God, and dark Zhoukoudian.

COME AND SEE US SOMETIME

People grow old, their quarrels cease
Dividing them, as the common fate
Kicks in. The man with the prize,
Ten books on the shelf,
The man you used to hate,
Turns out, against all odds, to be yourself.

The enemy you shrank from, a friend in disguise,
Turns to the wall and dies.
Too late, now, for the word to be said.
Let our dusts mingle
And be nothing. Let our headstones
Lean, at a charitable angle,

Into each other's space,
Conspiratorial, wise
Beyond the binary knowledge of the living
As a child comes, all eyes
For the future, through the maze
Of unforgiving.

TO THE PHILIPPIANS

And he humbled himself, obedient unto death
— Saint Paul

Open-eyed, she stares into the void,
Occasionally blinking, seeing nothing. Interrogative
You might say, but no longer of people,
Not at this hour, when the wards, the corridors
Are empty, and the Filipinas chat
In the nurses' station, and the stacked bags
Of human rubbish, bleeding on the floor,
Await removal. Slow, the movements of symphonies
Belly and pulsate, like jellyfish,
Through the weightless ozone. You would like to speak,
You have nothing to say. The sockets of her eyes,
And behind them, nothing. Was that a smile, a sigh?
And suddenly her loud enormous yawn
Unfettered by convention, declaring boredom
Absolute, collapses into silence
As the timeline straightens, systole, diastole,
Dead to the world again, unripples and flows on.
That was not a question in her eyes.
Acceptance is absolute. Matter reigns.
Write your name in the book of visitors,
A citizen of Philippi, in a declining age,
With the void staring back at you
And the road to Damascus nowhere traveled on.

TORONTO SUITE

It was unimaginable,
The freezing dark out there
Beyond room temperature
On the nineteenth floor—

My cubit of perspective,
Solitude. Far below,
The ongoing work of the ferries
In death-chill, darkness...

I was ripe for collection,
I and my dog-eared volumes,
Watching, as Lake Ontario,
Lost but for lights

That were islands of the blessed
On its waters, stopped
Like a clock without hands,
And only the hours went on,

The millions below in the lobby,
And the single heartbeat
On the ansafone, glow-dilating
In its votive space.

BALLINAFULL, 3 JULY 2014

Dermot Healy, 1947–2014

It was like an eye opening,
An eye, or a space
Between nature and itself —
And through it poured the days,

The years, the mountain-shapes...
There was a smell of hay,
And swallows, elbowing their way
Between nothing and nothing,

Keeping the elements open wide
And summer at the full.
In the high corner of a field,
On this side of the wall,

A human crowd, a passing bell.
This being Ireland, sea in the distance,
Wind and skies, the changeable —
In short, existence

On the latch, or the hook,
Like a sashed country window,
An eyelid, or an inch of light
Propped open by a book.

DEATH'S DOOR

Christ, the weight of that coffin. And the plot
So bottomless from above, is overflowing
With generations. There it is, the root
Of every dark emotion — down there, growing.
Please, can I die now? Tired, I straighten up,
The whole of life behind me, all my dead
From Antofagasta to Luton, Cargin to Bray Head,
Adding to themselves, as nothingness
Weighing a ton, and biting like a strap
Against my shoulder, shucks itself off. The river
Has become a strait, and the race of men
Is changing into gods who live forever.
Standing back, I make a Sign of the Cross,
And death's door shuts against me once again.

GOODBYE TO CHINA

Stripping for death not love,
I lose myself in the Chinese crowd.
We have no shame,
There is nothing to prove,
And none of us needs a name.

Everything has been said before
In this or another language.
Steam surrounds us, we are ghosts
Resurrected from self-image,
Clothes on a bath-house floor.

An earth-gnome, batlike ears
And giant phallus, gives me the eye.
Where are the women now, I cry,
My Xiaoqin, my Wenming Dai?
Where are all those years?

We are setting out, a host of souls,
The fiction of gender
Behind us, the pathos of roles—
Of time and distance, Xian, Chengdu,
Of passports and controls,

The pathos of history, Sichuan strikes,
Of railwaymen in 1911,
Stevedores in Shanghai,
Of Mao Tse-Tung and Chou En Lai
And dreams of an earthly heaven.

Setting out, we are setting out
Past Xinchan range
And Lingquan temple, time and change,
Forbidden City, Tiananmen,
After the end, before the beginning

Brings us round again—
An accidental brush of lips
At Beijing airport, one winged seed
I keep inside the leaves of a book
For just this hour of total need

And zero expectation
All I can cling to, conjure with
All I have with which to grow
Tomorrow, through another death,
Another incarnation.